To
Bonnie & Peter

From Tom and Barb __ God Bl__

(they are some
friends of ours
in England)

December, 2005

For: Julian

Maybe someday, you will explore the beautiful
land of great Britain. Wales has some lovely scenery —
and lots of sheep.

With our love,
Grandad and Grandma

DISCOVER

# A Shepherd's Year

### Beverley Birch
### photography Nick Birch

## SIMON & SCHUSTER

LONDON • SYDNEY • NEW YORK • TOKYO • TORONTO

To Oswald and Idris Jones and John Owen,
and the many other
sheep farmers of the Conway Valley

First published in Great Britain in 1990
by Simon & Schuster Young Books

Simon & Schuster Young Books
Simon & Schuster International Group
Wolsey House, Wolsey Road
Hemel Hempstead HP2 4SS

Printed in Great Britain by

BPCC Paulton Books Limited

British Library Cataloguing in Publication Data
Birch, Beverley
    A shepherd's year.
    1. Wales. Livestock. Hill sheep. Shepherding
    I Title
    636.3'08'3

    ISBN 0–7500–0002–3
    ISBN 0–7500–0010–4 pbk

# CONTENTS

The snows have come early this year. Bitter winds are sweeping across the mountain ridges, and damp mists drift in the upper valleys.

It is only the end of September. But already our sheep feel too cold in these wild Welsh mountains. Through the warmer summer months the flocks have been roaming the high pastures happily. But it is time to take them down to the shelter of the valleys.

The day of the winter gathering in the mountains is hard. We left our farms before dawn and climbed fast to the mountain ridges where the sheep graze. It is a long trudge, and you need to hunch deep in your coat against the bite of the wind.

To the north, west, south and east, other farmers climbed from their farms, their sheep dogs running eagerly beside them. By dawn we stretched in a long line across the ridges, driving the scattered sheep together in a great column of animals. Down through the passes we brought them, towards the old stone walls of this sheep fold in the lower valley.

By mid-day the sheep are all in. We take a moment for a quick drink and some food before the heavy work of the afternoon.

In the next hours we sort the animals. Sheep from fifty different farms are milling around the fold. We must separate them, and each of us take our own flock down to the home farm. The ear markings tell us where each sheep belongs. Sometimes they have strayed from a far distant farm, and we must return them.

As the hours go by it becomes muddier, and colder, and wetter. But you have to work on steadily, handling the sheep so they are not injured or frightened.

We must finish well before nightfall. Ahead of us there is still the journey down to our farms.

It is good to see the other farmers. Most of us farm alone, and we don't come together very often. There's a chance to swap news and gossip, just as our fathers and grandfathers did before us, at this same fold, in the years gone by.

## Winter

Here in the mountains even summer sunshine can turn in minutes to treacherous mists and rain. There is little shelter from the wind which chills you to the bone.

And even lower in the valleys, it is a harsh place to farm. The sheep have to be strong and hardy to survive. And our dogs, too, must be tough. They have to tramp the land with us, in wind, rain and snow,

checking the flock, nosing out the sheep that may be injured, or trapped, or falling ill.

There are busy months ahead, preparing for winter. We have fences, walls and gates to mend, hedges and ditches to check. As the deep winter sets in we move the flock into fields much closer to the farm. It is more sheltered lower down, and easier to reach them in very bad weather.

9

# Winter

November is tupping-time, the mating season between the female sheep, the ewes, and the male sheep, the rams, with their great curling horns.

In the weeks that follow there is a lot to do. The sheep must be kept healthy and well-fed, producing sound, strong lambs in the spring. Small lambs have a fight to keep warm, and in these parts spring can be a cold, wet time.

All kinds of illnesses from germs, worms and pests can attack the sheep. Diseases may kill a growing lamb inside the ewe, or cause it to be born before it can live outside her body. We protect the flocks as much as we can with vaccinations, dosing and dipping with medicines.

Through these dark winter months there is little grass. We give extra food, hay, root crops like swedes, and foodstuffs made from cereals such as wheat, maize, barley and oats.

And all the time we watch over the pregnant ewes. As February ends and March begins, we move them right up to the farm. There is still not enough grass growing, so we take food each day.

11

# Spring

There isn't much sleep for any of us, once lambing begins, just the odd few hours, fully dressed, napping in a chair. Throughout the day and night we must check on the ewes and the new-born lambs.

You can tell when a ewe is going to give birth. Restlessly she moves around the field. She looks for a sheltered place. She lies down, gets up, lies down again . . .

The labour pains get worse. She starts to strain, pushing the lamb out. You musn't fuss or worry her, just be near in case she needs help. Sometimes the lamb is too large, or isn't lying head-first, and then the ewe needs a little gentle, quick, careful help.

The new-born lamb drops to the ground. At once

the ewe gets up and turns to lick it. Lick, lick, nudge, lick, she forces it to its feet, massaging with her tongue. A shake of the head, and the lamb struggles up. It is only minutes since it was born. A few minutes more and it is suckling at the ewe's udder.

A new lamb must get milk straight away, or it won't live. Sometimes a ewe dies in lambing, and we must find another ewe to suckle the lamb. If twins are born, we hold them close together so they smell the same and the ewe will take both.

13

## Spring

Cold, starvation, foxes and hunting birds may kill an unprotected tiny lamb. The ewes must be kept strong and healthy, producing plenty of rich milk. Then the lambs will grow quickly and survive cold, wind and rain.

As April ends and May begins, the grass is growing on the mountains again. The lambs are older,

beginning to graze a little. They are ear-marked so we can recognize them, and protected by vaccinations against disease.

They are strong enough now for the pastures at the top of the mountain. In a few months they will stop taking milk from their mothers, and only graze the new spring grasses.

15

## Summer

By May the ewes and young lambs are on the mountains, roaming freely, grazing the grasses which grow richly in these milder weeks. But even now the summer is often not warm. Sun can give way to rain and mists in a few treacherous minutes. With the dogs we must climb to the tops every few days to check the flocks.

Around mid-summer, we gather them again. We need them down at the farms for shearing. The sheep's wool will fetch a good price from the wool merchant.

16

At this time of the year most of the sheep are on the mountain, and the gathering is enormous. Some farmers come from sixteen kilometres away. We set out on the long, steep climb before dawn, so that by first light we are already driving the sheep together. The dogs run eagerly on all sides, rounding up the strays and catching the stragglers. We must not lose any of the young lambs.

Within hours thousands of sheep stream down the mountain to the fold.

17

## Summer

We always take boots and coats against the sudden storms. But this year the weather holds fine and hot, and it is thirsty work sorting and separating the sheep. Some of us have brought small camping stoves to brew a pot of tea. Others settle with flasks and sandwiches. There are tit-bits for the dogs, and a run to a nearby stream for a long drink.

In the afternoon there is a sudden dark mist, upon us and past again in minutes. The sun shines on.

18

The dogs struggle to get into the fold, but we order them to the tops of the walls. They watch eagerly. There seem to be some sheep from another area. We don't recognize the ear marks, and need the book of marks to check.

It is nearly dusk of the longest day in the year before most of us are homeward bound with the sheep. Some flocks will have to stop halfway at nightfall, and go on towards home only the next morning.

19

# Summer

Shearing begins a few days later. You need warm, dry weather for shearing. If not, losing the wool coat can be a terrible shock to the sheep. It may even then kill them.

Once the weather is right, shearing must be done with speed. You don't want to fuss the sheep, but handle them calmly, shear the coat, or fleece, and let the sheep run free at once.

It is a difficult skill, learned only with much practice. The shearer must cut the wool evenly, not damage the sheep's skin, and remove the fleece in a single large sheet. He turns the animal gently with his legs and knees, holding the cut fleece back as he moves the shears in long sure strokes.

Not many farmers do it themselves. A well-cut fleece can be sold for a good price to the wool merchants. Spoiled fleeces are almost worthless. Usually a few farmers learn the skill, and travel round, shearing at one farm after the other.

Everyone in the family helps. Quickly a sheep is brought from the pens, the area swept clean of twigs and straw, the fleece sheared, folded, rolled, tied with the neck wool twisted into a rope, put in the wool sack. Then on to the next . . .

The wool from our Welsh mountain sheep is coarse
and strong. It makes good coats, carpets and blankets,
and in this wool-mill they like it because it is so tough.

When it reaches the mill, it has to be changed from the raw fleece into threads which can be woven. It is a long process from our fleece to a brightly-coloured woven blanket.

The wool is tossed and loosened. Then they feed it into the 'tenter hook willey'. This has a drum with teeth sticking out which straighten and open up the fibres of raw wool.

The carding machine rubs the raw fibres into threads which are wound on to long spools. Next they will be spun – the threads stretched and twisted slightly, to make a stronger, continuous thread.

# The wool story

The spun wool is wound into long, loose circles of wool called hanks, for washing and dying.

They are put through the wash. Clean, they can be hung on rods and lowered into great baths of dye – purple, green, red and brown, brilliant blues and yellows.

The weavers must decide the pattern of colours they want in the weaving, and set the machine. Now the wool is ready for weaving. At this mill they make splendid bedspreads and blankets in rich, deep colours. They may have as many as 2450 threads.

The shuttle shoots the cross threads between the others held tight by the machine. The weaver raises and lowers these to make the interwoven pattern of colour, as the shuttle races across as many as 95 times a minute.

## Summer

On the farm, work goes on. With shearing over, it is time to dip the shorn sheep and kill the pests which live in the wool. Pests can be very dangerous, even killers. At this time of year blow-flies are a bad problem. They lay eggs in the wool. Within days the eggs change into larvae which burrow into the skin and cause terrible pain.

Each sheep must be put in the dip for a minute, long enough for the fluid to soak right through the wool.

They don't like floundering through a deep trough of strong-smelling liquid. They shake themselves violently, and rush out as fast as they can.

As July begins the flocks are sent up the mountain slopes for the rest of the summer weeks . . .

28

Autumn is here, and the time of the sheep-sales. We sell our older ewes to lowland farmers for breeding. The ewes are too old now to stand our icy winters. Later in the month there will be more sales, when the ram lambs are sold.

We need to get a good price for the animals. It is an anxious day, listening to the auctioneer taking the price bids from the farmers. Some are selling, some are buying.

It is also a chance to exchange news with friends. Some we haven't seen since the autumn sales last year.

# Winter again

The days are getting shorter and colder. Already there is a winter chill to the winds, and the mountains take on their harsh, forbidding look again.

30

It is time again to bring the sheep down from the mountain. Just as last year, and the year before that, we prepare for the winter gathering.

And soon it will be tupping-time again . . .

# Word list

**auctioneer** (page 29)   The person who controls the buying and selling at an auction. This is a kind of sale where people 'bid' for the price they will pay for something, and it is sold to the person who makes the highest bid.

**dipping** (page 10)   Dipping the whole sheep into a bath or trough of medicine, to kill pests which live in the animal's wool.

**dosing** (page 10)   Giving a measured amount of medicine by mouth.

**germs** (page 10)   Microscopic living creatures, too small to be seen with the naked eye, which cause disease if they invade a human or animal body. The general name for all microscopic living creatures is microbe.

**labour pains** (page 12)   The pains that happen during birth.

**pests** (page 10)   Small creatures, such as ticks, mites and fleas which live on an animal, causing discomfort and illness.

**suckling** (page 13)   Sucking milk from the mother.

**vaccinations** (page 10)   Putting germs which have been weakened or changed in some way into an animal's body. This forces its natural defence system to fight off the disease usually caused by those germs. If live, active germs of the same kind enter the animal's body, it is already prepared against them.

**worms** (page 10)   The kinds of worm that live in the stomach of an animal and make the animal ill.